BABES IN CHRIST

SESSION 7

EVANGELISM and DISCIPLESHIP
INTERFACING

DR. AARON R. JONES
Foreword by Dr. Timothy M. Hill

Interfacing Evangelism and Discipleship

WORKBOOK

Babes in Christ

Dr. Aaron R. Jones

Interfacing Evangelism and Discipleship – Babes in Christ

Copyright © 2018 by Dr. Aaron R. Jones

Printed in the United States of America

Published by Kingdom Publishing, LLC, Odenton, MD 21113

All rights reserved. No part of this book may be reproduced or transmitted in any form or by any means, electronic or mechanical, including photocopying, recording or by any information storage and retrieval system without written permission from the author, except for the inclusion of brief quotations in a review.

All scripture quotations are from the King James Version of the Bible. Thomas Nelson Publishers, Nashville: Thomas Nelson, Inc. 1972

Editor: Sharon D. Jones

Graphic Designer: Janell McIlwain – JM Virtual Concepts

        Tiara Smith

ISBN 978-1-947741-22-5

Table of Contents

Interfacing Evangelism and Discipleship Sessions 1

Foreword 2

1 Peter 2:2 Paradigm 3

Understanding the Babe in Christ 5

Babes in Christ Experience the "New" 9

      New Creature 10

      New Family Relationships 13

      New Eternal Home 16

      New Inheritance 19

About the Author

Contact Page

Interfacing Evangelism and Discipleship
Sessions

Session 1—**Introduction and Philosophy**

Session 2—**5 Principles to Encourage Evangelism**

Session 3—**Components of Evangelism**

Session 4—**Bait for Evangelism**

Session 5—**Methodology of Evangelism**

Session 6—**Church Planting Produces Evangelism and Discipleship**

Session 7—**Babes in Christ**

Session 8—**Components of Discipleship**

Session 9—**Evangelism and Discipleship Plan**

Session 10—**Spirit of Forgiveness**

Foreword

When God calls a man of faith and fortitude to a specific purpose in the building of His Kingdom, He uses an individual like Dr. Aaron Jones.

Feeling the urgency of the hour, Dr. Jones has shaped his participation in the FINISH Commitment by emphasizing the merging of evangelism and discipleship strategies to assist churches and individuals in their quests to effectively reach the lost. As Senior Pastor of New Hope Church of God, he is well-aware of what it takes to affect the Great Commission of our Lord.

Dr. Jones' desire is to instruct others on how to deliberately make an impact on winning souls and then discipling them for powerful Christian service. His all-inclusive approach will intrigue and provide the impetus for those willing to pursue the heart of God.

Interfacing Evangelism and Discipleship will change the course of your outreach!

Dr. Timothy M. Hill
General Overseer
Church of God, Cleveland, Tennessee

1 Peter 2:2 Paradigm

1 Peter 2:2 Paradigm

As newborn babes, desire the sincere milk of the word, that ye may grow thereby:"

_____
_____
_____
_____
_____

Interfacing Evangelism and Discipleship – Babes in Christ

- The Greek word for "babe" is "nepious"
- Infant
- Little child
- Untaught
- Unskilled

_____
_____
_____
_____
_____
_____
_____
_____

Understanding the Babe in Christ

Understanding the Babe in Christ

- When we are born again, we become spiritual newborn babies (John 3:1-8).

___
___
___

Interfacing Evangelism and Discipleship – Babes in Christ

- The need for milk is a natural instinct for a baby, and it signals the desire for nourishment that will lead to growth.

_____
_____
_____
_____

- Once we see our need for God's Word and begin to find nourishment in Christ, our spiritual appetite will increase. We will start to mature.

_____
_____
_____
_____

- You need the milk of the Word of God.

_____
_____
_____
_____

Understanding the Babe in Christ

- The Father's food is the Word of God.

- Children tend to grow up and want to do adult things.

- Babes in Christ want to grow up to be like Jesus.

Interfacing Evangelism and Discipleship – Babes in Christ

- Continue to pray that your appetite for God's Word grows daily.

- The Benefits of Milk

- God's Word has the necessary ingredients for you to grow.

Babes in Christ Experience the "New"

Babes in Christ Experience the New

- New Creature (II Corinthians 5:17)
- New Family Relationships (Ephesians 2:19)
- New Eternal Home (II Corinthians 5:1)
- New Inheritance (Romans 8:17)

New Creature

"Therefore if any man be in Christ, he is a <u>new creature</u>: old things are passed away; behold all things become new."

II Corinthians 5:17

- This new life comes from the Holy Spirit.

_____

_____

_____

- You are beginning a new life under a new Master.

_____

_____

_____

Babes in Christ Experience the "New"

■ No longer under Satan's influence/control

___

■ You are enjoying a fresh start.

___

Additional Notes

New Relationships

"Now therefore ye are no more strangers and foreigners, <u>but fellowcitizens with the saints</u>, and of the household of God."

Ephesians 2:19

■   We are in God's household.

_____

_____

_____

■   We are experiencing spiritual blessings.

_____

_____

_____

Interfacing Evangelism and Discipleship – Babes in Christ

- We have new privileges.

_____

_____

_____

- God is your father (Romans 8:15).

_____

_____

_____

Additional Notes

New Eternal Home

"For we know that if our earthly house of this tabernacle were dissolved, <u>we have a building of God</u>, an house not made with hands, eternal in the heavens."

2 Corinthians 5:1

■ John 14:1-6

_____
_____
_____

■ Jesus is the Contractor and Builder.

_____
_____
_____

Babes in Christ Experience the "New"

- Something every believer should look forward to seeing

_____

_____

_____

- Where we will dwell forever

_____

_____

_____

Additional Notes

New Inheritance

"And if children, heirs also, <u>heirs of God and fellow heirs with Christ</u>, if indeed we suffer with Him so that we may also be glorified with Him."

Romans 8:17

■ Co-worker

_____
_____
_____

■ Temporary pain

_____
_____
_____

- Everlasting glory

___

- Great reward

___

Additional Notes

About the Author

DR. AARON R. JONES serves as Senior Pastor of New Hope Church of God. Under his pastorate is New Hope Kiddie Kollege, Inc (Daycare) and New Hope Community Outreach Services, Inc. Dr. Jones also oversees New Hope Church of God Ghana (2 churches) and New Hope Church of God Uganda (3 churches).

Dr. Jones is an Ordained Bishop with the Church of God denomination and is the DELMARVA-DC District Overseer (16 churches). Dr. Jones serves on DELMARVA-DC's Regional Council, Ministerial Internship Program Board, Urban Ministry Committee, Finance Committee, and Chaplain's Board. He also serves on both the Church of God's International and DELMARVA-DC Ministry to the Military Board. In his local community, Dr. Jones serves as a Chaplain for the Charles County Sheriff Department. He also serves as Board Secretary for the United Ministers Coalition of Southern Maryland, Inc.

Being obedient to 2 Timothy 2:15, "Study to show thyself approved…," Dr. Jones received a Doctorate in Theology and Pastoral Counseling from Life Christian University and a Doctorate in Christian Counseling from American

Christian College and Seminary. He is a certified Pastoral Counselor with the International Association of Christian Counseling Professionals. He is a Life and Pastoral Coach. He is the former Executive Vice President of the National Bible College and Seminary in Fort Washington, Maryland.

Dr. Jones has published ten books and a soul-wining project that provide a biblical foundation for Christian doctrine and discipline. He has recorded a CD entitled, Peace in the Storm. He is the founder and owner of God's Comfort Ministries, LLC, which provides Christian literature, evangelism training, and spiritual guidance. He has appeared live on TCT Network; WATC-TV's Atlanta Live; Babbie's House (hosted by CCM artist Babbie Mason); and In Concert Today on DCTV. He has done radio interviews with Radio One's WYCB's program; The Praise Fest Show; and online with Total Prayze. He was featured on the cover of Change Gospel Magazine and interviewed on Promoting Purpose Magazine.

Dr. Jones not only serves God, but his country as well. He has served over 20 years in the Armed Forces. He is a retired Chaplain with the Army National Guard. He participated in both Operation Noble Eagle (2003) and Operation Iraqi Freedom III (2005).

Dr. Jones is happily married to the former Sharon Russell. He sincerely believes without her love, support, and encouragement, many of his goals would not have been accomplished.

Contact Page

Mailing Address:

150 Post Office Road #1079

Waldorf, Maryland 20604

Website: www.godscomfort.net

Email: drjones@godscomfortmin.net

Facebook: God's Comfort Ministries

Twitter: @GodsComfort_Min

Instagram: @godscomfort_min

GOD'S COMFORT MINISTRIES

God's Comfort Ministries (GCM) provides practical Christian books, teachings, trainings, and coaching to new converts and seasoned believers. GCM provides understanding of the doctrinal principles of the Bible.

Services Provided

Pastoral and Life Coaching

Evangelism and Discipleship Training

Spiritual Guidance

New Author Consultation

Christian Literature

www.ingramcontent.com/pod-product-compliance
Lightning Source LLC
Chambersburg PA
CBHW081358080526
44588CB00016B/2537